MONSIGNOR WILLIAM BARRY MEMORIAL LIBRARY
BARRY UNIVERSITY
PS3556.L284 N44
Flaig, Phyllis M.   010101 000
Neither chart nor cross : poe

0 2210 0074480 7

Y0-CJG-014

PS
3556
.L284   119139
N44

Msgr. Wm. Barry Memorial Library
Barry College
Miami, FL 33161

FLAIG

NEITHER CHART...

NEITHER CHART NOR CROSS

PHYLLIS M. FLAIG

Neither Chart Nor Cross

THE GOLDEN QUILL PRESS
Publishers
Francestown   New Hampshire

Barry College Library
Miami, Florida

© THE GOLDEN QUILL PRESS 1978

Library of Congress Catalog Card Number 78-58283

ISBN 0-8233-0277-6

Printed in the United States of America

DEDICATED TO

My beloved children, Phyllis June Tyndall and Major Donald W. Flaig (ret.) and to the late Vivian Laramore-Rader, Poet Laureate of Florida, who trained me, and to Gilbert Maxwell and Dr. Hans Juergensen who encouraged me.

ACKNOWLEDGMENTS

The author gratefully acknowledges permission to use certain of these poems which were first published in the following books or magazines: *The Ladies' Home Journal, Kaleidograph, Lyric* and others.

Many thanks also to the Poetry Societies who have given awards to many of these poems and published them in their Year Books or in Anthologies: The Poetry Society of Georgia, Poetry Society of Pennsylvania, State Poetry Society of New Mexico (Anthology), Laramore-Rader Poetry Group, World of Poetry Anthology, University of Miami Chap Book and New American Speech - used in schools in two states, Texas and Wisconsin.

CONTENTS

Refugee	15
Winds of Chance	16
The Gulls of Mona	18
The Castle	20
Enigma	22
Fantasia	23
The Listener	24
Girl With Blue-Black Hair	25
I Must Tame the Wildcats	26
Ballad of the White Hand	28
Edna St. Vincent Millay	30
Afternoon Tea at Osborne House	32
On the Death of My Blind Father	33
Girl With Amber Eyes	34
As Grows the Seed	35
Gateway to Understanding	36
In Time of Drought	37
On Seeing Navajo Sand Paintings	38
Zuni Chant for Spring	39
The Legend of Comanche Creek	40
No Fences for Na-Wah-Ka	42
Winter Episode: A Twice Told Tale	44
Exodus from Big Cypress	46
Prairie Woman	47

University Library 9:30 P.M.	48
House of Thirty Doors	49
Berry Picker	50
Scars of Sorrow	51
Duty Weaves a Harsh Net	52
In a 16th Century Garden	54
Hill Woman	55
Call of the Low Country	56
Grapes for Figs	57
End of an Interlude	58
Beethoven: Man of Fury	60
This My Wilderness	61
The Street of Cats	62
The Room	63
Man by the River	64
Bonkei Garden	65
In a Japanese Garden	66
Progeny of Fire	67
Neither Chart Nor Cross	68
Mountain Music	69
American Monument	70
The Dreamer	71
First Heartbreak	72
Great Adventure	73
Blind Child	74

De Profundis	75
Ten Years on an Island	78
Blue Gazelle	80

INTRODUCTION

What is there to say about the beautiful, forthright lyrical work of Phyllis Flaig? These poems, so smoothly executed as to seem effortless, are, to my certain knowledge, the end result of painstaking, arduous labor by a woman who is a true poet rather than merely a highly accomplished versifier.

The pieces which deal with a most unusual storybook childhood enchant the discerning reader with clear-cut landscapes and compelling portraits of close family members, nannies, and aged eccentric relatives. Mrs. Flaig works with precision within the confines of brief lyrics and with equal effectiveness in the freer forms of verse. Poems of the Navajo, their customs and tribal heritage seem to have been written by someone who has lived intimately and sympathetically for years with these stoic, proud and reticent people. Perhaps though, the best thing to be said about this brief book as a whole is simply these poems bear the stamp of individuality to a marked degree. At times their direct simplicity deceives us, but make no mistake about it; such simplicity is arrived at only through the devious labor of working and reworking line and phrase to achieve a crystal clear, free flowing effect of natural spontaneity.

If I have any complaint at all about the contents of this book, it is this: as a proud, self-reliant incredibly courageous human being who has outlived more tragedies of physical and emotional agony than anyone I know, this woman has chosen not to use these experiences as grist to her mill.

I like and admire the poetry that she has written. I also hold in higher esteem than mere words can convey the humorous, consummately brave human being who is and will always be my good neighbor and truly understanding friend. When you have read this book, you will have had a glimpse of the person I love and admire. Beyond that I can say only, from the depths of a grateful heart, that I am sorry for everyone who is not privileged to know this exceptional woman who seems always, to me, to be surrounded by an aura of rainbow light.

GILBERT MAXWELL
Miami, 1978.

NEITHER CHART NOR CROSS

REFUGEE

I had not thought
one drop of blood
or bone in me
had understood
or cared to touch
forgotten earth,
or see again
my place of birth.

Yet when these fields
are April green,
or harrowed earth
smells fresh and clean,
something awakes
a memory
as of the lost
once dear to me.

WINDS OF CHANCE

It was a gusty wind of March
that brought me to my mother's bed
although she did not want a child
and nine months lived with dread;
but April came . . . and May . . . and June
followed by moons that turned to years
and through young childhood I was dressed
in handmade garments of the best,
but cloaked in lonely fears.

Then a wind of adversity came
sweeping throughout the house;
he whirled a Bacchanalian dance
and when he left there was no chance
of ever again wearing silks and laces
or taking a trip to foreign places.
Gone were the gardeners, maids and cook;
the stables had a desolate look,
and since my mother's joy was pinned
to a life demolished by that wind,
her days were full of tears.

As I grew too old for childish play
I still believed what winds could say;
then a summer zephyr, kind and warm
brought me a lover who took my arm
and led me away to a dream-built land
where he bound me fast with a golden band
and jewels in my ears.

Then I heard a wind with sorrow tell
that there would be a funeral knell,
and hearing it I stayed beside
my loved one till the hour he died.
All my life the winds have swept
across my path. Sometimes I wept,
yet if they call me I shall know
and follow in silence wherever they go.

THE GULLS OF MONA

As a child of seven I lived alone
in an ancient house of quarry stone;
My parents had died . . . there were few who cared
how an only child of seven fared.
Transient nannies prepared my food
and watched my manners were not too rude;
they combed my hair and washed my face
and one from duty taught me grace
and fear of an angry God above —
but no one ever showed me love.

Yet those fleeting days when I was seven,
through all my life have interwoven
tapestries of gorse-grown hills
and quiet valleys where daffodils
and bright forget-me-nots grew wild,
and I was allowed, though just a child
to roam at will. There was no telling
how far it was to the nearest dwelling —
perhaps twelve miles, but that was why
the women who cared for me would not stay.
Yet I was not lonely . . . how could I be,
companioned by gulls who flew in from the sea?
Many a morning I woke to their call
as they drifted like snow to the rock-built wall.
They waited for me and one was so tame
he flew to my shoulder when called by name.
I believed their chatter brought tales from the sea —
No, I was not lonely . . . how could I be?

But that was so many years ago
and where it was I scarcely know;
today, in my house not far from the sea
I hear gulls calling . . . but not for me,
and I am so lonely for one small haven
and all I believed as a child of seven.

THE CASTLE

It must have once belonged
to some unlordly knight
whose royal grant was meager
compared to those bestowed
on paragons of chivalry.
It was an unpretentious place
(which castles seldom are)
but it had dignity that mocked
its origin in feudal times.
The granite walls climbed tower-high
and looked down with pride
upon a small triangular isle,
formed by three rivers
whose sluggish waters joined,
like old women holding hands
to make a circle; this had been the moat,
but age had given it to frogs,
croaking their nightly messages
to cousins who preferred
their more secluded bogs.

The castle could not boast
of faded tapestries, nor armor
glaring facelessly from shadowed halls;
if they had ever lent their grace
it was an era no one could remember.
But there were bounteous treasures
never wrought by human hand;
the grey stone bridge showed crevices

where gillyflowers grew, their velvet petals
painted with mahogany and gold;
their fragrance that of cinnamon.
Along the river banks cowslips nodded
to king-cups rising cleanly out of swamps;
primroses shared the field
with Queen Anne's lace and hawthorn
blossoms drifted down like snow.

I have never known regret
that for one cherished year
this ancient dwelling was my home;
I did not miss conveniences
nor comforts that I now demand . . .
Although it was a period
of intermingled poverty and bliss,
I found contentment there.

ENIGMA

This I never mentioned
but sometimes I believed
I must have been a foundling
and I had been deceived,
or why would one whose mother
was more than circumspect
ignore the woman-things
a daughter should reflect?

Instead, I ran through heather,
wind riffling unbound hair
and raced through stormy weather
forgetting every care . . .
Yes, I must be a foundling —
how else could one explain
empathy with wind,
affinity with rain?

FANTASIA

Somewhere in childhood's shrouded mist
I lost the place where "Good-morning" kissed,
I watched a woman take fresh-baked bread
from an oven. While it was warm she spread
thick slices with butter and all were laced
with plump brown raisins, closely spaced,
and yet my mother said today
that this was all a fantasy:
she never had baked one loaf of bread —
then whence came ambrosia that I was fed?

Long before I became a man
I stood on a shore where wild tides ran,
and I saw a vessel whose use was spent,
her mast was broken, her keel was bent.
She lay on her side in a wind-locked cove,
known only to me and the gulls above;
but my father says I have never been
anywhere near such a dismal scene.

My parents were old when I came their way,
and once in the night I heard them pray:
"God pity the child who came out of the sea."
Did they mean me . . . did they mean me?

THE LISTENER

If you should walk with me
through an empty house
would you call it fantasy
or the skitter of a mouse
if I became aware
of heels that tapped the floor
or thought I heard a hinge
creaking on a door?
Would you even dare
to scoff at muted laughter
and the swish of brocatelle
that brushed against me after?
Would you be unwilling
to admit a faint perfume
suddenly pervaded
the dusty vacant room?

If this be so, then please,
leave without a word —
Go! and let me listen
for a voice once heard.

GIRL WITH BLUE-BLACK HAIR

I have come down from the mountain
where a young girl stood,
slim and straight as a dryad
in her native wood.
Her limbs were pale as a silver birch
and smooth as a sapling tree
but I only saw her pale smooth limbs,
her face was hid from me
by her hair, her long black hair,
her tangled blue-black hair.

She could have held in the cup of her hand
a heart that yearned for her
but she looked across the valley
and kept on combing her hair,
combing her hair, her long black hair,
her tangled blue-black hair.

I have come down from the mountain,
what happened no one knows,
but dry leaves cling to my arms
and crushed ferns to my clothes,
and what of the dryad who stood by her tree?
She promised to come down and marry me . . .
and twined through my fingers
my bramble-torn fingers
are strands of her hair, her long black hair,
her tangled blue-black hair.

I MUST TAME THE WILDCATS

    Why can I never forget
    dark memories, hiding
    like little wildcats
    waiting to pounce again.

I can remember my mother
clutching the hand of her little son
as though he were the answer
to her unsolved problems.
We three were crossing a field
on our trek to the sea;
it was greener than emeralds
and starred with wild flowers,
but she never noticed . . .
the field had no answers.

The sea, angry that day,
attacked the rocks in fury,
but the rocks knew they were eternal,
they were still unharmed
after millions of tempests,
but that was no comfort to my mother
who had her own tempests.
She stamped her feet
until tears of frustration
fell like dewdrops, gulped by sand.
She was bitter . . . so bitter
because she no longer knew
what the misted future would hold —
but do we ever know?

She was based on this island
with only peasant fisher-folk
as neighbors, and none she would talk to.

My father was away . . . somewhere,
trying to pick up the fragments
of their life style but he was not bitter —
that was not in his nature.
If the sun ever shone on my childhood
the rays came from my father,
and the wildcats in my mind
slept quietly, deeply,
when we were together;
but my mother looked constantly
at her fingers denuded of jewels
and fed the wildcats with bitter bread.
Age did not mellow her, although
my father found most of the pieces,
but a broken vase, though carefully mended
is never as precious as it once was.
That was eons ago, but I am still trying
to tame the wildcats and their kittens
so they will scratch no more.

BALLAD OF THE WHITE HAND

The Mistress of Buffington Hall left instructions that at her death her right hand was to be severed and buried separately from her body, because with it she had signed away part of her beloved ancestral estate.

The winds that strip the oaks of leaves
pass through with sorrowing moans,
but those who hear them every year
insist their monotones
are not the winds, but weeping
of the Mistress of Buffington Hall;
they say she haunts the grounds at night
and some have heard her call:

"O Hand, white hand whose perfidy
once signed away my heart,
if at last I shall find rest
our graves must lie apart."

Some say she strolls beneath the trees,
across the weed-choked ground
to where a sculptured marble hand
marks a lonely mound.
They say on autumn nights she walks
across ancestral land,
a scarf of mist about her wrist
bare of the guilty hand;
and when the winds moan round the hill
or cry along the lane

the shivering old women say,
"Milady walks again."

"O Hand, white hand whose perfidy
once signed away my heart,
even in death I find no rest
although we lie apart."

EDNA ST. VINCENT MILLAY

1

Harsh blew the wind you knew when you were young,
cruel the sting of ice in winter air,
the breath of sea was brine upon your tongue
but summer's honey always lingered there.
Your voice was like the murmuring of pines
or as the sand that sighed beneath your feet
yet there was pathos in your written lines
as of one lonely on a crowded street.
How much of that bleak coast you knew, became
identified with your impulsive youth?
How could austerity of region claim
to be your heritage? There is no truth
in that, for neither ice nor rock could be
remotely traced in your heart's ancestry.

2

You lived with hunger greater than the need
for bread and meat, you felt a deeper thirst;
your spirit groped through darkness as a seed
reaches for sun although its root is cursed.
Your heart was desolate; love came no more
and if arms briefly circled you at night
it was a game and left no warmth to store
since disenchantment came with morning light.
Then later years brought one with wine and food
to satisfy all unfulfilled desire,
to comfort you . . . to talk . . . or if your mood
demanded it, to sit beside the fire —

and now with thirst and hunger gratified
you thought your haunting wraith might be denied.

3

Insistent was the knock upon your door;
alone, you went to let the caller in;
although he had come visiting before
he had not seemed so pale nor quite so thin.
This time he came to tell you of his grief:
That there were few who welcomed him at all
but held to life as autumn's tattered leaf
still clings and flutters for an interval.
You took his hand in yours as if to share
his secret, but he kissed your brow and left
without a word. No sound was anywhere;
you sighed that those you loved would feel bereft
when they were told that you were found at night
lying upon the floor . . . and not one light.

AFTERNOON TEA AT OSBORNE HOUSE

They said she was a dear old lady,
that great, great-aunt of mine,
but I remained completely silent
not wishing to discuss her personality
that cloyed and sickened me
when I was far too young
to be tolerant and kind.

Her little cap of rose-point lace
rested precariously on dangling curls,
no longer grey but yellowed as the pages
of an ancient book, and just as dry
against my face, as she held me tight
with bony arms sleeved in black silk,
hugging me so that I could not slide
from her slippery satin lap.
She smothered me with kisses
and stifled me with gardenia perfume;
then, as usual, she asked me to sing
my little French songs. Because I was shy
I hated her . . . Oh, how I hated her . . .
but they all thought she was a dear old lady
so I crawled under the tea table
and sang the songs.

ON THE DEATH OF MY BLIND FATHER

Why do I feel no grief
who loved him so
and watched him wither
like an autumn leaf
in winter's snow?

Why do I shed no tears
though winds of death
blew over him?
He had no fears
of their kind breath.

How can I borrow
solace through weeping,
knowing he will see
with clarity tomorrow
when he awakes from sleeping.

GIRL WITH AMBER EYES

She always wore her amber beads,
not purchased from a shop in town
nor ordered from a catalog
to grace a non-existent gown;

No one bequeathed them in a will
her relatives were simple folk
who scorned frivolity in dress
so . . . of the beads she never spoke.

The curious often asked her if
she bought them while she was away
or if they were a gift of love —
She pursed her lips and would not say.

Just once she said, to their surprise,
"Somebody thought they matched my eyes."

AS GROWS THE SEED

I was your first love. Long before you knew
life's meaning I supplied your every need;
It was my body that first nourished you,
I was warm earth to slowly waking seed.
Born into light your flesh had new design,
the seed had found its way into the sun,
yet love in other forms would follow mine,
feeding the growth of what I had begun.

But when another comes to take my place
I shall not turn to you with tear-dimmed eyes
nor hold you in the lock of my embrace
and pray my love has taught you to be wise.
I was your first love, Child, but some bright hour
the seed I cherished will put forth its flower.

GATEWAY TO UNDERSTANDING

I am no kin to Running Deer
but I have known this Navajo
as though he were my brother.
He has taught me many things
about his people; their chants;
their legends and shrouded traditions.
I have heard poetry in their spoken words
and share their sensitivity
to all the spirit world.
They feel the rhythm of a flowing stream;
the whispering of wind stirred leaves;
They see the changing colors of the mountains
as painting from the hand of the Sky Father
who showers them with abundant gifts
but warns them these must not be squandered.
       He gives them corn for sustenance;
           herbs for healing; animals for meat
              and skins for winter clothing.

Running Deer believes if he goes searching
with the eyes of his belief, he will find
footprints of Elder Brother, son of Sky Father,
who will lead him in his twilight
to the Far Beyond above the highest peaks
       where he will dwell forever
          with his forefathers
              in the peace of the Blue Land.

IN TIME OF DROUGHT

No gentleness
pervades this land
where a brassy sun
scorches its brand.

Rooted in rock
a withered tree
will die without
fertility,

and vultures wheel
to pause in flight
where cattle skulls
lie starkly white.

Straying sheep,
raw-boned and sore
bleat beside
a hogan door.

A Navajo
stands tall and straight,
his stern-lipped face
accepting fate

for in this land
his seed was sown,
it is his sinew,
heart and bone.

ON SEEING NAVAJO SAND PAINTINGS

Remember, my brothers, remember
when you danced beneath the White-Masked Moon;
recall the promises of the Rainbow Goddess
and the tales of the Blue Rain People
who support the sky and move all within it.
Revive your spiritual poems, painted with sand,
and when the clinking coins of cities call
let them not close your ears
to the Chant of the Little Stars.
Forget not the Whirlwind people of the desert
nor the four butterflies who followed
a pollen trail to a spring of clear water.
Tell your sons the ancient legend
of the coyote who stole a flame from the Fire God
and carried it to First Man and First Woman.
Hold fast, my brothers, to traditions,
and teach your children to revere the Old Ones
who were blest by the gold light of morning
and danced beneath the White-Masked Moon.

ZUNI CHANT FOR SPRING

O Sun above the mountains,
gild their peaks with living fire
that Old Ones shivering in their years
may feel your warmth again.
O fair White Moon across the valley,
paint the clouds with silver light,
that those who live with pain
may know your healing power.
Warm Rains, fall gently now
upon the newly planted seeds
that they may drink clear water,
and winter-hungered people
will eat their fill of tender corn.
O Winds that are the breath of gods
blow gently on the trees
whose swelling buds may break their bonds
and clothe the branches with green leaves.

Great Spirit, we who are your sons
chant this prayer for Spring
who wakes the world to new life
and blesses all within it.

THE LEGEND OF COMANCHE CREEK

Comanche Creek is not a joyous stream,
leaping and gurgling when spring ice breaks,
instead it grumbles angrily,
pounding on sleeping rocks
as if it were a predator
gnashing at bare bones.

Natives say when earth was young
and men believed all living things
were host to spirits, blest or damned,
that there was once a tribesman
who harbored a demon in his mind,
enjoying the evil power it displayed.
The whole tribe called upon their Holy Man,
and begged him to relieve
their brother of his curse.

The Shaman came in priestly garb,
with eagle feathers round his head
and sacred stones about his neck.
Within his buckskin fetish bag
were eyes of frogs and ears of dogs
and charms that none had ever seen.
For seven days and nights he prayed,
intoning the ritual Chant for Health;
on the seventh night a white masked moon
blessed the tribesman, and he was healed,
as a dark and writhing creature
slithered into Comanche Creek

and was never seen again;
but since the night of that white moon
no fish have lived within the stream
nor are the waters safe for drinking.

NO FENCES FOR NA-WAH-KA

An old, old woman stood by the corral,
fingering her turquoise beads
as if they were a rosary.
Her skin was the tint of autumn leaves,
her eyes as dark as blackberries
and her face lined like a network
of roads on a modern map.
While she watched the mustangs
her lips were muttering
in a strange and guttural tongue,
low and born of resentment,
"You don't know the things I remember;
you are too young, but I saw your fathers
racing across the valleys . . . proud and free;
their unshod feet clicking on stray rocks;
their manes flying loose
in winds from the mountains.
There were no fences then . . . My people
were happy, too, in their freedom.
We lived our way, believing in spirits
who lived in trees and in the waters
of streams, and in all creatures on earth.
We knew our gods and talked to them
and they advised us wisely,
but if we angered them they punished us
by sending sandstorms, thunder
and the fire of lightning.
Now we are no longer free to roam
but live as though imprisoned by a fence.

Our children do not care to hear
the legends told by grandfathers
nor are they willing to talk to gods."

A ranch hand stood near the old woman
and called angrily to Na-Wah-Ka,
"Leave the mustangs alone;
you upset them with your damned crazy talk.
Get back to your sons . . . and stay there."
Only the faint print of her moccasins
showed where she had been
as the old woman shuffled away,
but she would not return;
Na-Wah-Ka was going
where there are no fences.

WINTER EPISODE: A TWICE TOLD TALE

It was winter when Coronado and his men,
searching for a mountain pass,
came upon a village of six hundred souls,
who lived in peace and grew their maize
and built small dwellings of adobe blocks.
How could the Great Explorer ride
behind a cross while greed and violence
filled his heart and influenced his soldiers?
The Indian men who only killed for meat
to supplement the things they grew,
were murdered in the name of God,
perhaps the same one that they knew.
With swords the soldiers slashed
one foot from every woman,
yet all were forced to serve as slaves
while children hid in fear.

The Spaniards stayed all winter through,
desires fulfilled by sullen women
who could not help themselves.

When spring came to the village
there were no plantings of potatoes;
no corn; no squash, and no men to hunt
so starving women and the children died.
Coronado and his men rode on
to claim more land for Spain
and search for gold to fill their saddle bags
to enrich themselves, the church and king.

The story now is told again
where lonely houses and a kiva stand,
recently unearthed
from their protecting sand.

Told to me by the archeologist who was in charge of the "dig".

EXODUS FROM BIG CYPRESS

In the style of a Scandinavian poem from which Longfellow borrowed the form for "Hiawatha".

This is a place of many waters,
silent, murky deep swamp waters,
oozing through the cypress forests,
seeping under mangrove thickets,
creeping slowly to the sea.
Here are coots and great anhingas,
purple gallinules whose pecking
wakes the sleeping alligators,
lying motionless as tree roots;
swift-winged herons, egrets, ibis,
white as flowers of the moon vine,
come to rest on jade leaved branches;
frail wild orchids sway in rhythm
to the dirge that wind is playing
on his harp of marsh-grown sedges,
as he mourns forgotten warriors,
as he wails for bronze-skinned hunters,
sadly leaving this fair haven.

PRAIRIE WOMAN

Gaunt as the dry-leaved tree beside her door,
a woman scans the prairie parched for rain.
She sees great cracks like open mouths
then searches the sky for any sign
and prays again.

The plains have taken all she knew of youth . . .
her hair once shining like the silk of corn,
is drab as tassels wintered in the field,
and years of struggle have drawn facial lines
that winds have sealed.

Only her eyes are those of one with faith,
their depths are mirrors of her hidden strength;
beaten by nature's whims, emotion sleeps
until a lightning dagger rips the clouds,
then in relief she weeps.

UNIVERSITY LIBRARY 9:30 P.M.

Serious young architects
weighed down by stresses and strains:
embryo solons, drowsy as old judges;
long-haired poets, writing of life
      as they believe it,
        all nod over their books
and support heavy brows with fidgety hands.
They scratch their heads, pull their ears
or twist pencils in their nostrils,
oblivious to the room or to each other.

The door opens; a whiff of perfume
rouses them all from lethargy;
heads lift like the antennae of moths.
A girl beckons and a youth
with football shoulders
closes his books noisily;
        they leave together,
        the architects smirk,
        the solons yawn,
the poets return to their dreaming.

HOUSE OF THIRTY DOORS

No more shall I walk through those doors,
thirty doors that look upon
the darkest night, the brightest dawn
and mute the cry of wind-swept moors;
but I have stood beside each one

and, standing there, have heard the sea
beating time upon the rocks,
slapping boats against the docks
and always beckoning to me
by blowing salt-spray through the locks.

Yet thirty doors that creak and sway,
that stick and pull and open hard
or slam as if they meant to guard
those within, lest any stray —
all thirty now are locked and barred

to me by those behind the doors,
whose nights are safe within their keeping;
those who never heard my weeping,
those who swept their too clean floors
and thus erased me with the sweeping:

But once there was a man who dared
to show the world how much he cared,
and we would not have crossed the sea
if thirty doors had welcomed me.

BERRY PICKER

I saw her picking blackberries
with arms all briar-torn,
a livid scar along one cheek,
her grey hair closely shorn.
Although the brambles had cut deep
her heart knew greater pain
from tragedy that left a wound
never to heal again.

She had been a pampered child
whose father built her throne,
but all Pandora's imps
had marked her for their own.
Though she walked with head held high,
enduring torment with staunch pride,
those who knew her grief was deep
never once had seen her weep.

SCARS OF SORROW

There is no wound more cruel,
no anguish quite as deep
as grief I bear in silence
for one I love.
I cannot heal his sorrow
nor take away the pain,
although I suffer twice,
once for his wound
from a sudden thrust —
as with an unsheathed sword,
once for myself
who knows the source
but must not speak a word.

DUTY WEAVES A HARSH NET

I shall never forget Andria,
that golden-haloed Juno,
caught in a net of duty's weaving.
Her husband's lifelong grief
lies heavy on her heart
for when a child at play,
Rob maimed his younger brother,
and all the years between
has cared for this half-man,
warped in body and mind.
World-traveled Andria stagnates
in this place Rob long ago outgrew,
yet both stay on, targets
for arrows of insult,
hurled by a sodden cripple.

The old white-pillared house
once rang with laughter,
now only peddlars approach the door;
the air is tainted with disdain
of small-town mothers, since Robert
chose his bride from other fields,
scorning the local belles
in their cotillion days.

Behind the shuttered windows
Andria dreams a clammy hand
is at her throat, but dares not think
that shackles would be loosed

if one frail wretch should die.
Only in her crimson room is she alive,
revived by color of her choosing
and by the gentleness of Robert's love.

IN A 16TH CENTURY GARDEN

Her garden was a radiant thing,
blazing with color of an English spring
but Anne was lonely.

She walked where gilliflower and larkspur grew
and where like sentinels the hollyhocks
stood guard above the lupins and the phlox
but Anne was tasting bitterness of rue.

Was there such beauty in London
where Will spent so much time?
Were there mignonette and foxglove?
Could yellow roses climb
upon the dark wall of a town?

Carefully lifting her somber gown,
Anne kneeled to pick forget-me-nots
and pressed them to her tear-wet face.

HILL WOMAN

Burned by sun,
weathered by wind,
her face is lined,
her body thinned.
The years that sculptured
her frame in bone
have yielded little
to call her own
yet she is hardy
as hillside weeds
whose roots grow deep
to find their needs —
but she lifts her eyes
and drinks her fill
of serenity from
a quiet hill.

CALL OF THE LOW COUNTRY

My mother often told me of her land
where marsh grass waged a constant war with tide,
yet wove a net of roots beneath the sand
where frightened crabs could scuttle in to hide.
She told me how the winter wind would roar
and lash against the ocean's heaving breast;
she spoke of how the gulls would wheel and soar
and where the little terns used shells to nest.

Because she loved the low land she was sad
that I had never known its changing mood —
but we had left when I was just a lad,
too young to understand it as I should;
But somewhere in my being is a seed
my mother must have planted in her need.

GRAPES FOR FIGS

But they shall sit every man under his own vine and under his fig tree and none shall make them afraid. — MICAH 4:4

From the childhood of time
men have dreamed dreams of peace
and forgotten them . . . and dreamed them again;
but even in the days of forgetting
seeds of Micah's vision have been kept alive
in the hearts of poets and simple men:
The belief that earth is still a garden
where men shall sit as brothers
each beneath his own tree . . . without fear.

But the rains come . . . or come not . . .
the sun burns angrily or not at all
and the winter slashes with knives of ice
so that my brother's trees bear no figs
but I have grapes and we shall share them
until his trees fruit again.
Being a simple man, I do not ask
his usual income from the trees
nor if his neighbors are acceptable to me.
I only ask, "Has want lain by your door?"
and having appeased his hunger, I implore
that he in turn feed other men
and trespass not upon another's land
but keep alive the dream
that every man shall sit under his own tree
and none shall cause him to fear.

END OF AN INTERLUDE

Frederic Chopin to George Sand

You still believe my love is all for you,
as it should be, whose resolute devotion
has eased my days. I would that it were true
but love is not revived by any potion
such as you bring sometimes to warm my fingers,
yet when the light goes from my candle flame
remember that a part of me still lingers
within your arms, still murmuring your name;
but all my music with its undertones
breathes of my love for Poland; every chord
tells of her frozen tears, her martyrs' bones
more eloquently than the spoken word.
Forget that once we loved and on the morrow
think of Poland dancing in her sorrow.

George Sand to Frederic Chopin

I never thought your love was all for me
nor dared believe our liaison would last;
it was enough — our villa by the sea,
my books, your music, till your dark moods passed.
It was enough to urge the candle flame
to burn a little slower . . . save its light
and when the paroxysms of coughing came
to hold you in my arms throughout the night;
but now you hear the voice of adulation,
(transparent as the ruffles at your throat)
I pray it will not stifle your creation

nor bring to silence even one frail note.
Your love was not for France and not for me,
only for Poland . . . and a memory.

BEETHOVEN: MAN OF FURY

Forgive my fury! How can I refrain
from passion as this dread affliction creeps
upon me, stealing peace from nerve and brain?
Only a chord like crashing thunder sweeps
this demon from my ears. It soon will close
my hearing to all music but my own
and dare me in my silence to compose
another opus ... Am I turned to stone?
My music is my life; this complication
must not destroy the talent I have fought
to nourish through my years of deprivation;
the place I have attained was dearly bought.
These new dynamics are of terror's making
and only anger keeps my heart from breaking.

THIS MY WILDERNESS

I was an Esau
whose birthright was earth's bounty . . .
my mess of pottage — a few more hours of sun,
but now I cry in this my wilderness
and chase mirages of the beauty I have known.

Once there were apple blossoms
blushing with the spring's first surge
and Judas trees that splashed their flame
against the rain-washed skies;
Dogwoods embroidered the hills
with snowy fantasies
and where I walked wind flowers used to sway,
pale dancers in a pastoral ballet.

I was happy in the morning of my life
and wiser in my love of simple things,
but now I cry in this my wilderness
and chase mirages of those kinder springs.

THE STREET OF CATS

This should have been like any Monday —
busy after a lazy Sunday
but the sky was dull and the window pane
was showing the first faint spatter of rain.
This was a day to pause and remember . . . .
Suddenly I was back in September
as a student in Rome, on a narrow street,
(hidden away from the tourist beat)
on the street of cats whom no one owned,
some sleek and proud and some raw-boned.
>   There were hungry cats
>   and angry cats;
cats as sly as noxious vermin
and cats whose coats were white as ermine;
>   curious cats;
>   furious cats;
kittens like tigers with orange fur
and shy little things just learning to purr,
but they fought and scratched and climbed the trees
then jumped from the branches to balconies.
At twilight the peasants brought scraps of meat
from their masters' tables for cats to eat.

While I painted, an artist with glowing eyes
watched me, to help and criticize —
though he spun elaborate dreams instead
and coaxed me to share his life and bed —
but I was not willing and sailed for home,
far from the artist and cats of Rome.

THE ROOM

When midnight came Matilda slipped away,
her death as unobtrusive as her life,
and he who never had been one to pray
blasphemed the God whose hand had touched his wife.
Her clothes were left as though she might return,
her toiletries all thrust into a drawer;
without her faith the old man could not learn
to live with grief, but closed and locked her door.

No life again would enter, he believed
and sealed himself within a coat of ice,
but when he joined her, those who came perceived
the room had been a habitat for mice
and spiders hung their filaments inside . . .
for life was there that could not be denied.

MAN BY THE RIVER

For years we knew the old man could not see;
we marveled that his white cane found this place,
we often wondered what could possibly
bring such contentment to his placid face.
He surely did not know that sunlight danced
across the river where the willows start,
nor could he watch for stars nor be entranced
when sudden moonbeams tore the clouds apart.

But we forgot . . . or did not know the truth —
that he whose eyes no longer walked with light
had cleared this wooded path in early youth
and traveled it a thousand times at night;
now he sees things that we shall never see,
all captive in his undimmed memory.

BONKEI GARDEN

Hands like old ivory,
with nails work-broken
planted this garden as a token
of affection for a son
as yet unborn.
Firmly they pressed
into a soil-filled bowl
a dwarfed and twisted yew,
some moss, a stone or two . . .
a pair of figurines . . .

For sixty years the tree has lived
yet only briefly knew
the son's expected care . . .
the well-loved first-born,
whose shroud was sewn by war;

But I, who came as enemy
and stayed as friend,
learned to love and earned the love
of those old ivory hands.
Now in my bonkei garden
the figurines still stand,
reminder of another day,
another land
and one benign and smiling face —
a mediator for his race.

IN A JAPANESE GARDEN

It was no dream, though dreams have captured it
and bound it to my heart with silver thread;
it was no fantasy though earth and stone
were clothed in silk when cherry blooms were shed.

Chiseled from rock, the terraces kneeled down,
making obeisance to the spring-blessed trees,
an offering more reverent than prayers
a vested priest chants on his Sunday knees.

A rustic bench beside a white-flecked pool
was where we once had pledged undying love —
then there was rubble where the garden grew
and one tree left, whose burned limbs rose above

the ravaged earth. Now scars are healed again
and lovers walk beneath young cherry trees;
they seldom ask about the blackened walls —
they know why holes pit all the terraces,

but each year when the fragile blossoms blow
I shall return . . . and wonder if you know.

PROGENY OF FIRE

Prometheus who stole the heaven-born flame
could not foresee the dangers of its might;
to him it was a force dispelling night —
a treasure of the gods from whence it came.
He could not know that men would learn to tame
its power, and in taming find delight,
using its strength to forge and to ignite,
forgetting that unharnessed it could maim.

If he who lay in anguish on the rock
had seen the issue of his hard-won prize
propelling missiles into outer space
he would have guessed that Zeus would only mock
attempts of men to violate the skies
or laugh, as though at pygmies in a race.

NEITHER CHART NOR CROSS

No stone marks cities tombed beneath the sea,
embalmed by centuries of salt and sand;
their sodden walls are angled crookedly
and shudder at the current's least demand.
The rose has given way to ocean fern
and scarlet-tipped anemones bright plumes;
through gaping windows strange fish dart and turn,
crustaceans make their beds in empty rooms.
The lost Atlantis, deaf to rosaries
kneels at the mute "Engulfed Cathedral" door
where only phantom priests pray on their knees
for postulants who come to them no more
and Undine, combing out her long white hair
searches in vain to find a lover there.

MOUNTAIN MUSIC

Can there be any
lovelier thing
than the pizzicato
of a mountain spring
where pale fern tendrils
gently mock
impenetrable
mounds of rock?

Stray winds wander
from the distant seas
to pluck harp music
from exiled trees.

A falling branch
with sudden crash
re-echoes like
a cymbal clash.

The whistling lad
whose flute-like note
springs from his young
untutored throat
is wholly
unaware that he
plays obbligato
to a symphony.

AMERICAN MONUMENT

There is a church whose Gothic walls
stand as a National Monument
to those who lie within its halls —
an ever living testament.

A laborer's many hours were spent
smoothing mortar on each stone
until his ageing back was bent
and time took toll of breath and bone.

Just one ambition gripped this man,
(Italian-born and poorly schooled)
since in his mind he had a plan
it was this thought alone that ruled:

That his Maria . . . "she so good"
should someday rest beside the great.
Untaught, he had not understood
it was for those who lie in state.

Humbly he voiced his dream aloud
only to have his hope denied;
he plodded on with dark head bowed
but plans long-fostered had not died.

Maria passed on . . . his sad heart stirred,
SHE WOULD NOT SLEEP WITH THE UNKNOWN
Cremated, now she lies interred
in mortar binding stone to stone.

THE DREAMER

I found her cloistered in a narrow room,
swathed in a blanket to defy the cold,
oblivious to life as if a tomb
imprisoned her; however I was bold
enough to rouse her from her fantasy
and urged her to accept the world I knew,
although Pandora's imps, in jealousy
would scoff at dreams that she believed were true.

Had I the power to reverse the clock
I would not waken her nor yet presume
to take her to a world that cynics mock
but I would beg to share her cell-like room
where Milton told her of his failing sight
and Shelley's dripping clothes made pools of light.

FIRST HEARTBREAK

Paul was such a guileless lad
with features like Adonis had,

his skin was golden from constant sun
and firm straight legs were born to run.

No one could throw so swift a ball
or climb a tree as fast as Paul;

yet no one knew as well as he
where early trilliums ought to be

or bees swarmed in a hollow log
overhanging the cranberry bog.

Paul had rabbits and three small goats
and a basket of kittens with soft gray coats;

I was a pigtailed child of ten
and he was my knight and hero then

until my mother scolded, "Such goings on!
I forbid you to play with the trash man's son."

GREAT ADVENTURE

When the last call comes and I must go
play no dirges and songs of woe
but cradle me down where the lupines grow
and I believe that I shall know.

When skylarks swiftly take to wing
and morning wakes to songs they sing,
as earth feels the pull of roots that cling,
they and I will know it is spring.

When the first pale gold of a daffodil
brings joy to the valley, and over the hill
the gorse and heather soon will spill
I may not see but my spirit will.

So, to those I loved: Do not grieve,
I shall learn so much more after I leave.

BLIND CHILD

She stands at the edge
    of a deep abyss,
bewildered and lost
    in uncertainties.

Reaching her hands
    to grasp the moon
she is unaware
    her path is hewn

from crumbling ground,
    and always she
gropes between dreams
    and reality . . .

Yet a gentle touch
    can guide her feet
to a place where earth
    and moon-world meet.

DE PROFUNDIS

No one knows the battle
I fought at Shipwreck Bay,
No one watched but gulls
and soon they flew away.

****

I was the child my mother bore
after her zeal was chilled . . .
It was because of me
her tired heart was stilled . . .
I was the one who closed
the door against her love . . .
I was a scar my father
touched with a sterile glove.
I lived in a world of my own,
companioned by wind and trees
until a greater need
propelled me to the seas,
but often in the night
I heard a strange voice say:
"Follow the wind and stand
alone at Shipwreck Bay."

But Shipwreck Bay is a fable
of which old sailors speak —
a pause in the path to adventure
that soldiers of fortune seek.
To me it was just a legend,
for no one I ever knew

had seen the place or dared
believe the tales were true.

One death-filled night my ship
was lost near Shipwreck Bay . . .
Again I heard the voice
as I heard my own lips pray;
scarcely alive I called
for help as I reached the shore
but only an echo answered,
dimmed by the thunderous roar
of tide as it beat against
immovable granite spires
in a vain attempt to mold them
after its own desires.

On the beach lay salt-pocked cans,
empty bottles, broken crates,
hingeless trunks, legless chairs
and the bones of vertebrates.
A seaman's cap and blouse
were hung on drifted wood,
erect as though saluting
as their wearer might have stood.
The painted wheel of an oxcart,
the seat of a farmer's wagon
leaned on a skeletal piano
with keys like fangs of a dragon.
The treasures of storm-tossed ships
cast up by angry waves

were drenched with the tears of men
lying in sodden graves.

The only sounds were the sea
and gulls on freckled eggs
and rats that squealed with hunger
as I fought them from my legs;
the gulls . . . the rats and the voice
with the words it used to say:
"Follow the wind and stand
alone at Shipwreck Bay."

Two months I nearly starved
till a freighter rescued me . . .
Two months I foraged with rats
in the stench of rotting debris.
The beat . . . beat . . . beat of the surf
was a pendulum in my brain —
but I learned to stand alone
and the boy became a man.

TEN YEARS ON AN ISLAND

I lived ten years as a lonely child
but to every day I was reconciled;
I could not imagine another world
where girls and women, powdered and curled,
went shopping for lace and pastel satins
while I never went to school or matins.
I had no companions except my brother
and he was the angel who worshipped my mother.
Both of them were extremely bored
by the things I loved, and both abhorred
the monotony of the restless sea
around this island, dear to me.
I knew no children to call by name
but birds and wood-creatures who were tame
surrounded me when I was alone;
I loved each tree . . . each curdled stone
once born of fire; I loved the sand
I dribbled through a rock-scarred hand;
I knew a dark precipitous cliff
where loud-tongued gulls assembled as if
to warn those who tried in vain to steal
their brown-splotched eggs for an early meal.
I tasted one once, (not stolen by me)
but the gift of an old man, retired from the sea.
I suppose there were some who thought I was wild
since I wandered about like a gypsy child,
but my father taught me to read and write
and to work on arithmetic every night;
then my grandmother took me away to school

where I learned to live by a rigid rule;
but all my life I have been content
to remember the treasured years I spent —
ten years with trees . . . with rocks and gulls
where I harvested knowledge not taught in schools.

BLUE GAZELLE

I never saw a unicorn
but once entranced, I stood
where a young gazelle
frolicked in a wood.

Her coat was blue as heaven,
her antlers gold as sun
and on her silver hooves
four jeweled anklets shone.

We romped till shadows lengthened
and I trudged home but there
my mother asked why ferns
were matted in my hair.

Child-vision is illusive,
once lost will not return
but if this was a dream
why the fern?